$5.00

910
CUL
Cullen, Derek
Exploring the land

DATE DUE			

PATHFINDERS
IN EXPLORATION

Exploring the Land

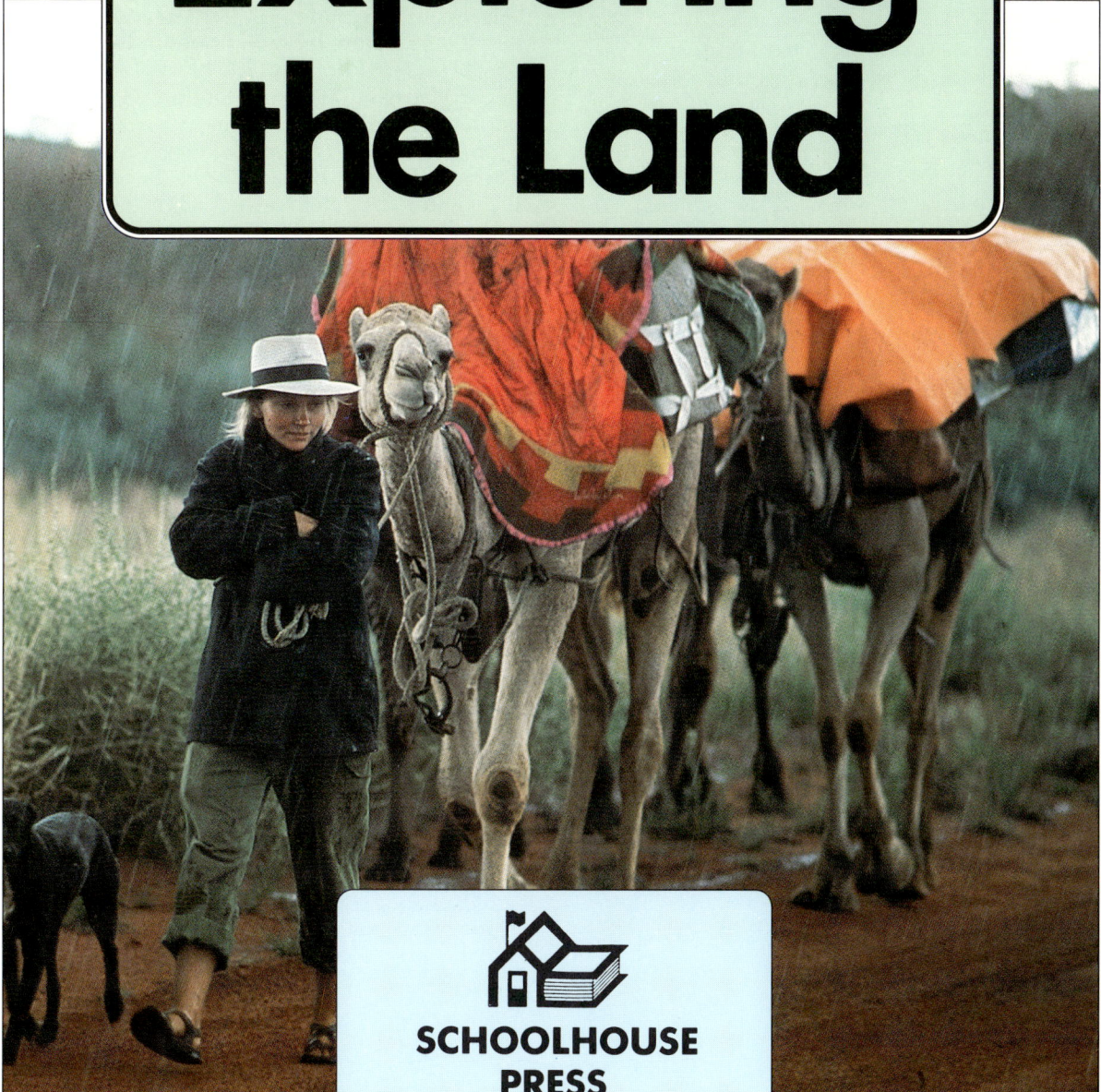

SCHOOLHOUSE PRESS

Authors: Derek Cullen and John Murray-Robertson

Designed and typeset by The Pen and Ink Book Company Ltd, London

Illustrated by Gecko Ltd

Picture research by Faith Perkins

Printed in Hong Kong

88/89/90/91/92/93   6 5 4 3 2 1

Photographic Credits

t=top b=bottom l=left r=right

The author and publishers wish to acknowledge, with thanks, the following photographic sources: 20, 40*t* J Allan Cash; 16, 19*r* Barnaby's Picture Library, London; 39*b* BBC Hulton Picture Library, London; 9*b* (Weidenfeld Archive) Bibliothèque Nationale, Paris; 7*b* (ms Bodl.264 f.239v), 9*t* Bodleian Library, Oxford; 23*t* Church of Jesus Christ of Latter Day Saints; 42, 43 Colorific; 19*l* Denver Public Library, Western History Department, Colorado; 15*b*, 27*b*, 33*l* and *r*, 34*t* Mary Evans Picture Library, London; 13, 23*b* Robert Harding Photograph Library, London; 34*b*, 37*l* Mansell Collection, London; 38, 39*t* Middle East Collection, St Antony's College, Oxford; 51*l* and *r*, 7*t*, 8, 28, 29 Peter Newark's Historical Pictures; 10, 12*r*, 15*t*, 16, 16-17, 18, 21, 24, 25*t* and *b*, 27*t* Peter Newark's Western Americana; 6, 12*l*, 37*r* Picturepoint (UK); 41*l* and *r* Popperfoto, London; 11 Public Archives of Canada, Ottawa; 28-29 (Weidenfeld Archive) Royal Geographical Society, London; 30 (Weidenfeld Archive) Scottish National Memorial to the David Livingstone Trust; 32 (Weidenfeld Archive) United Society for the Propagation of the Gospel, London

Cover photograph courtesy of Colorific, London and Robyn Davidson

The publishers have made every effort to trace the copyright holders, but if they have inadvertently overlooked any, they will be pleased to make the necessary arrangement at the first opportunity.

Note to the reader
In this book there are some words in the text which are printed in **bold** type. This shows that the word is listed in the glossary on page 46. The glossary gives a brief explanation of words which may be new to you.

Contents

Introduction

Today, we know a lot about our world. We have maps and atlases which show us where distant lands are. We can travel easily and quickly by air, sea, and road. We can see on television how people live in faraway countries.

The explorers of the past have given us this knowledge of our world. They went on long journeys to faraway lands and wrote about the places they visited. Some of them went to look for new **trade routes**. They were looking for new places where they could buy and sell goods. Some people went to find treasure. Other explorers went to open up new lands for people to settle in.

The Silk Lands

Over 3,000 years ago, the people who lived around the Mediterranean Sea began to make the first voyages of discovery. Many of the first explorers were merchants, and all their journeys were concerned with trade.

▼ Three thousand years ago, many groups of people lived around the Mediterranean Sea. These people were the first traders. The Mediterranean was like a crossroads between the three continents of Europe, Asia, and Africa.

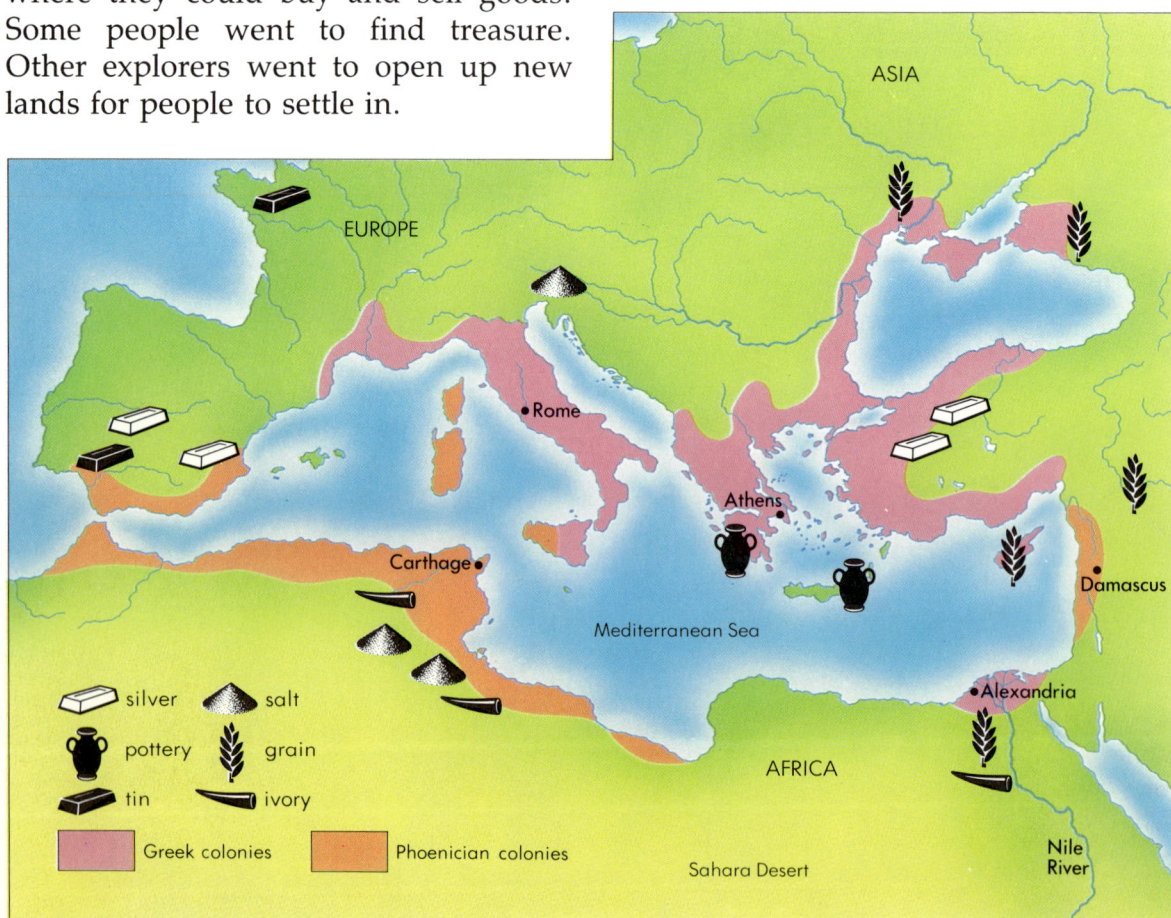

ASIA

EUROPE

Rome

Athens

Carthage

Mediterranean Sea

Damascus

Alexandria

AFRICA

Sahara Desert

Nile River

silver   salt
pottery   grain
tin   ivory

Greek colonies   Phoenician colonies

In the time of the Romans, new trade routes were opened up. Valuable goods, such as perfume, spices, and wood, were brought back from Asia, or the **East**, as it was called. A fine cloth called silk became greatly valued. No one knew a lot about the lands this silk came from. It was many years later that an explorer was to write about these Silk Lands of the East.

The Polo Family

In the 1200's, the Italian port city of Venice was a rich trading center. Merchants from Venice traveled widely and traded with the people from lands around the Mediterranean Sea. They bought goods from Arabs who had visited the lands of the East.

In 1254, two Venetian merchants named Niccolo and Maffeo Polo went to look for the riches of the East themselves. At that time, there was a great **emperor** named Kublai Khan who ruled all of China. His **empire** stretched across Asia from the China Sea to the Danube River. It was called the Mongul Empire.

The Polos were away for almost fifteen years. They came back to Venice in 1268. Then, they made plans for a longer journey. This time, they took Niccolo's son, Marco, with them. Marco Polo was to become one of the most famous explorers of all time.

▼ Kublai Khan was the Emperor of China. His people called him "the wise Khan" because they thought he ruled so well.

▲ Traders from Venice traveled far and wide. Marco Polo belonged to a family of traders. The family traveled in China and throughout Asia. When they came home, Marco Polo gave an account of what he had seen in a book. The book gave details of cities, canals, rivers, ports, and industries.

Exploring Asia

Marco Polo was only seventeen years old when he left Venice in 1271, with his father and uncle, to travel to China. The journey took three and a half years. The Polos joined a group of traders who were traveling overland with their horses and camels. This group of travelers was called a **caravan**. They crossed dry deserts and high mountains.

Kublai Khan had given the Polo brothers a flat, gold plate, or **tablet**, when they had been in China before. When the Polos showed this tablet to the local rulers, they were allowed to pass through without harm. At last, the Polos arrived in Shang-tu, a city in the north of the empire. It was where Kublai Khan and his **court** went in the summer to escape the heat of the south.

Kublai Khan as a Ruler

Marco Polo thought Kublai Khan was a good ruler. He was kind to his people, and he kept grain in huge stores to feed them when food was in short supply. He looked after the poor people and the children who had no homes. But if people did not obey him, he was strict and punished them. The Khan's people treated him with respect. They lowered their voices even when they were a quarter of a mile away from him. They wore soft slippers inside his palace.

Kublai Khan sent people with his orders to all parts of his empire. He sent these people on horseback. Every twenty-five miles there were rest houses for the messengers. Across the kingdom there were 10,000 rest houses and 300,000 horses! The empire was a vast land.

◀ The Polos probably took about thirty days to cross the dry Gobi Desert. They would have traveled from water hole to water hole. Today, the Mongol herdspeople have to keep on the move when looking for fresh grass and water for their animals.

The Capital City

Kublai Khan was very rich. His capital city, Cambuluc, was large and splendid. Today, it is called Beijing. It had wide, straight streets and large squares. No city in Europe was as big and as well planned at that time. The city walls were forty-five feet high and stretched for twenty-five miles all the way around.

Kublai Khan had a beautiful palace where he lived. In it, there were many fine buildings called **pavilions**. There was a great hall where 6,000 people could sit and eat. People in the palace ate off gold dishes. On Kublai Khan's birthday, people from all over his empire came to greet him. They all wore jewels and fine clothes.

▲ Beijing may have looked something like this when Marco Polo visited it. It was Kublai Khan's winter capital.

▼ In his book, Marco Polo tells us that Kublai Khan held banquets in his palace. An English artist painted this picture of Kublai Khan's birthday. We can tell that he did not know what the Khan's court really looked like. He has made it look just like a European court.

Marco Polo's Travels

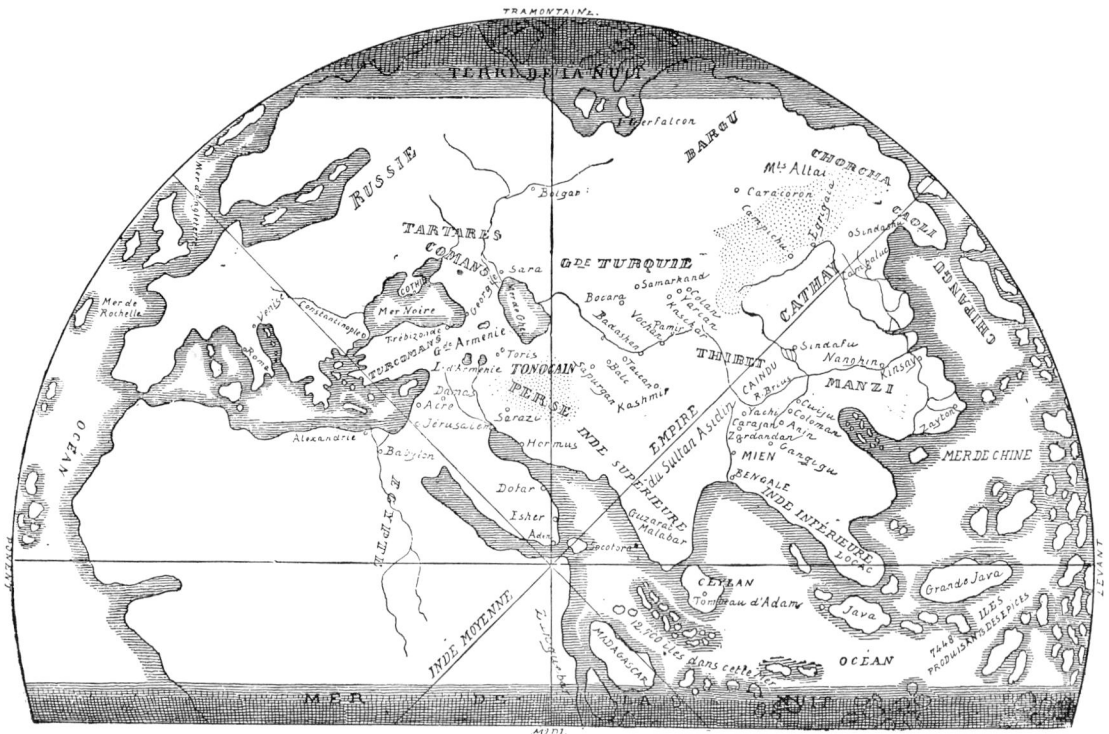

The World of Marco Polo.

▲ Travelers in Marco Polo's time did not know much about the world. They believed it was flat, and that it was dangerous to get too close to the edge. Many people did not believe that Marco Polo had been to the places he described. They did not believe that such places even existed.

Kublai Khan liked Marco Polo because he was young and smart. The Khan asked Marco to work for him, and he sent him on many tours all around his empire.

Marco visited many towns and cities on his travels. He even went as far as the borders of Tibet and Burma. He saw the city of Kinsai. This is now called Hangchow. Marco thought it was even more wonderful than Cambuluc. There were over one million people living there. It was a city which had **canals** like his own city of Venice. Everyone moved about the city in boats instead of horse-drawn coaches or on horseback. The people were friendly, peaceful, and honest.

Marco saw many things that amazed him on his travels. The Khan's people were printing books and using paper money. They were also using coal for heating. These things were not known in Europe at that time.

▼ Marco Polo saw many fine Chinese cities, including the city of Kinsai. In Marco Polo's time, Kinsai was a large city with more canals than Venice. Today, it is called Hangchow. The city is in the far eastern part of China.

The Journey Home

Marco Polo worked for Kublai Khan for seventeen years. Then, Marco felt it was time to return home. The Khan was pleased with his work and did not want to lose him. At last, Marco's chance came. Kublai Khan wanted to send a princess to marry a ruler in **Persia**. Persia was on the way from China to Venice. Kublai Khan asked Marco to go with the princess on her journey. They went by sea with fourteen ships. On the way, they stopped at the islands of Sumatra, Java, and **Ceylon**. When they reached Persia, Marco found out the ruler had died. The princess married the ruler's son instead. Marco also learned that his friend Kublai Khan had died. He was very sad about this news.

Marco Returns to Venice

Marco Polo was forty-one years old when he got back to Venice. He had been away from home for twenty-four years. People in Venice could not believe the stories he told of the strange land he had been to. They nicknamed him "Marco Millions" because they thought he was telling so many lies.

Three years later, Marco was taken prisoner in a war. In the prison, he told his story to another man. This man wrote a book called *The Travels of Marco Polo*. This book gave the best account of life in Asia for many hundreds of years.

▲ The Polos sailed across the Indian Ocean on the way home. People from Africa and Asia were sailing across the Indian Ocean all the time. Few Europeans made such long journeys.

9

Exploring the Canadian North

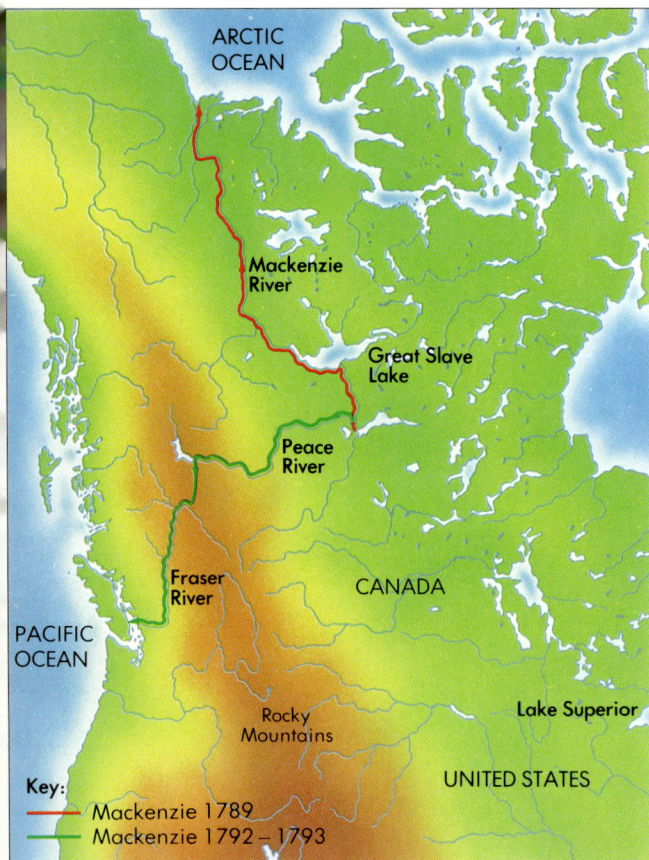

Key:
—— Mackenzie 1789
—— Mackenzie 1792 – 1793

◀ The route that Alexander Mackenzie took in his search for the Northwest Passage. He was looking for a route across the rivers and lakes of North America to the Pacific Ocean. His first attempt failed, but on his second journey he reached the Pacific on July 22, 1873.

The Young Fur Trader

Alexander Mackenzie was a Scot who had settled in North America. In 1785, he went to Lake Superior to trade furs. There, he lived among the fur **trappers** and learned about their way of life. The trappers lived like the Native Americans. They wore skins and furs to keep the cold out. They used canoes on the rivers and lakes to get from place to place. The local people who traded with Mackenzie called their land Canada. The trappers and settlers used the name, too.

▼ The trappers had to make long journeys alone through forests and along rivers. In a way, the trappers were all explorers. Alexander Mackenzie learned much from the trappers about surviving in the wilderness.

The journey east from Europe to China was a long and difficult one, so people also traveled west looking for another route. The first explorers crossed the Atlantic Ocean and found the **continent** of North America. They began to explore this land, and many people started to leave Europe to settle there. Some people settled near the Atlantic Ocean. Other people went farther inland to look for a way across America to China. They believed they could find a route to the Pacific Ocean through the lakes and rivers of North America. They called this route the **Northwest Passage**.

Looking for the Northwest Passage

Mackenzie wanted to find the Northwest Passage. In 1787, he moved farther west and settled there. There was another lake north of his new home called the Great Slave Lake. Mackenzie had heard of a big river flowing west from this lake. He wondered if this could be a way through to the Pacific Ocean.

▼ The earliest European travelers in North America were fur traders. They lived and worked among the Native Americans, trapping and trading for hides.

In 1789, Mackenzie set out with a large group, or **party**, of Frenchmen and Native Americans to find the Northwest Passage. They went by river to the Great Slave Lake. The water in the river was rough, and the weather was very cold. In places, the river rushed downhill over rocks. These parts of the river are called **rapids**. It is dangerous to travel through rapids by canoe. The men had to carry their canoes and all their supplies over the land to pass the rapids. When Mackenzie and his men reached the Great Slave Lake, it was frozen and they had to wait for the ice to melt.

North to the Arctic

When the ice melted, Mackenzie and his men found the river on the west of the Great Slave Lake. It was wide and flowed swiftly. The flood water of melted snow and ice swept them along. Their canoes often filled up with water.

The local native people in his party thought the hissing noise made by the rushing water was the voice of evil spirits. They believed that they would see big monsters. In fact, the only people they saw were the Inuit. The Inuit live in the far north of Canada and the US.

▼ An Inuit woman from Prince William Sound on the northern Pacific coast of Alaska. The Inuit made their clothes and ornaments from the hides and bones of animals.

When Mackenzie and his men reached the **mouth** of the river, they found a frozen sea. They realized they had reached the Arctic Ocean and not the Pacific Ocean. They had failed to find the Northwest Passage, but they had explored a 2,500 mile river. Today, it is called the Mackenzie River after the explorer.

▼ The canoes that Mackenzie's party used were the type that the Native Americans in the area used. They were light enough to be carried overland. They were also strong enough to hold several people in fast flowing water.

▲ There are mountains running all the way down the western side of North America. The longest and highest range is the Rocky Mountain rang. Mackenzie had to cross the Canadian Rocky Mountains to reach the Pacific Ocean.

Mackenzie Tries Again

In 1792, Mackenzie set out once again to find a way to the Pacific Ocean. This time, he went with nine men. They had made a canoe which was light enough to be carried by two men. It held ten people with all their food and weapons.

The men set out along the Peace River. It was hard work because they had to paddle up the river against the flow, or **current**. They saw herds of large beasts called moose. Ahead of them, they could see the snowcapped Rocky Mountains. The river began to flow more swiftly. Their way was blocked by rapids. The men cut a path through the trees, so that they could carry their canoe. The canoe was damaged many times.

The Pacific Ocean At Last

Mackenzie and his men met local native people who told the explorers which route to follow. They advised them to turn southeast where they would find a small river flowing to the west and the sea.

The men went on foot to the river, which is now called the Fraser. They followed this river to the Pacific Ocean. Mackenzie had made the first overland crossing of North America. On a rock by the Pacific, he carved these words: "Alexander Mackenzie, from Canada, by land, 22 July 1793."

The American West

Many European countries tried to claim America, but about 200 years ago, the people of America decided they wanted to be free. In 1783, they formed a new **nation**. They called themselves citizens of the United States of America.

At that time, most people lived near the east coast. For many years, no one explored farther than the Mississippi River. This river was the border, or **frontier**, of the country to the west.

In 1801, Thomas Jefferson became President of the United States. He wanted to find out more about the land farther west and to make it part of the United States. He was looking for the best way of traveling from east to west. He hoped there might be a big river which would allow people to travel easily across these large new lands.

The President chose two American soldiers to lead a group of men to find out more about the land to the west. They were Meriwether Lewis and William Clark.

▼ The route taken by Meriwether Lewis and William Clark. These two men were the first to cross the United States. They also explored the length of the Missouri River. As a result of their journey, our country began to expand westward beyond the Mississippi.

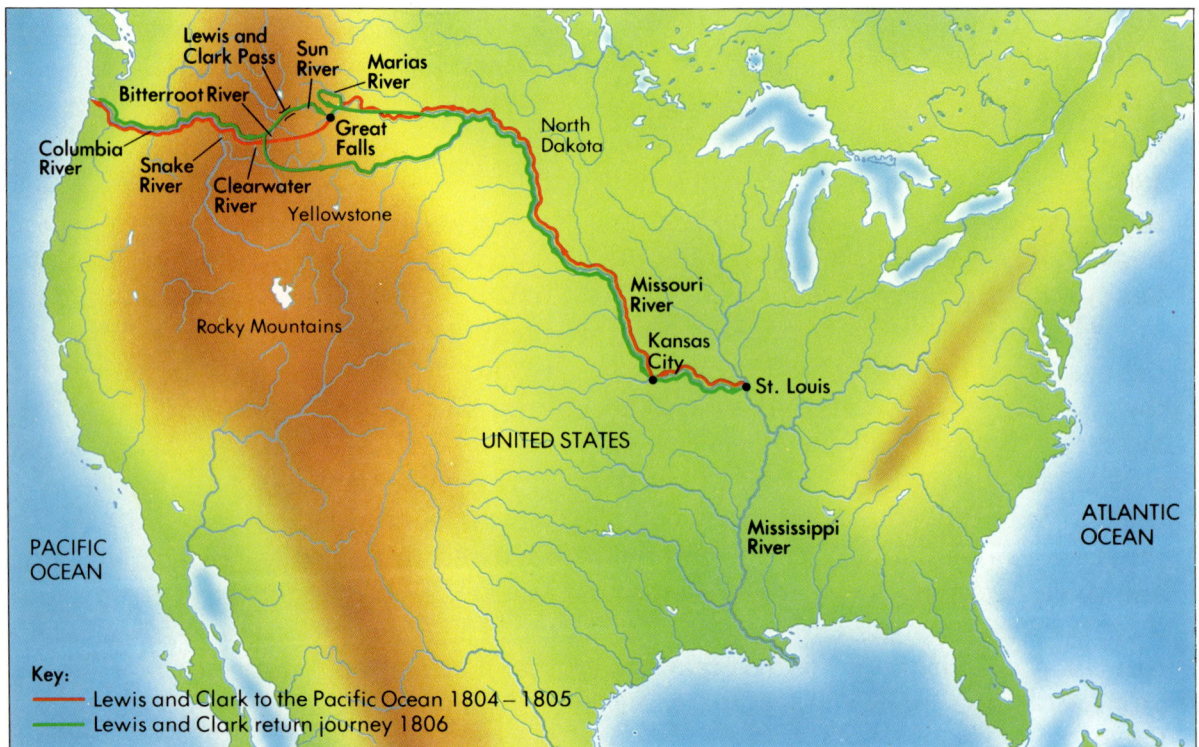

Key:
— Lewis and Clark to the Pacific Ocean 1804–1805
— Lewis and Clark return journey 1806

Getting Ready for the Trip

Lewis and Clark had been to distant, or **remote**, parts of the country before. They knew what they had to take with them. They built a boat which was about fifty-five feet long. It had to hold goods to sell to the native people. The boat also carried tools and weapons. Lewis and Clark took forty-five men with them. Many of the men were **blacksmiths**. Blacksmiths are people who make things from metal. There were soldiers, too, in case they had to defend themselves. It was a very well planned trip.

After they had started on their journey, Lewis and Clark met a woman from the Shoshone tribe. She agreed to go with them to guide them. She would help them to make friends with the people they would meet along the way.

Up the Missouri River

The party set off from St. Louis in May, 1804. St. Louis is where the Mississippi River joins the Missouri. No one had been all the way up the Missouri before. Lewis and Clark hoped to get a long way up the river before the winter. They planned to spend the winter upriver in the villages of the Mandan people. This area is now the state of North Dakota.

Their plan went well. The lower part of the river flowed through lands filled with animals to hunt and fruit to eat. On their way, they found a good place to build a **fort**. The buildings had a high wall around them to protect the men. Today, Kansas City stands in that place.

▼ Sacajawea was a Shoshone woman. She traveled with Lewis and Clark, and she worked as a guide and interpreter. Her husband came on the journey, too. He was a French-Canadian trapper. The couple took their little son along with them.

▼ The Mandan people lived in villages like these. By the time of the first snows in November, 1804, Lewis and Clark had found a good place to build their winter camp among the Mandan villages. They called it Fort Mandan.

Toward the Rocky Mountains

In the spring, Lewis and Clark moved on. They paddled their canoes farther along the Missouri River. They did not know that the high Rocky Mountains lay ahead of them.

They found one large animal that they had not seen before. It was the big and fierce grizzly bear. Lewis called it "the yellow bear." They killed the first bear with one shot. The next bear nearly killed them. It chased them until the sixth shot finally killed it! After that, they were much more careful about grizzlies. When one of them chased Lewis, he climbed a tree to escape. He escaped from the bear, but not from one of his men. Lewis was dressed in an animal skin. One of his men thought he was a bear up in a tree and shot him in the leg!

The Great Falls

The melting snow and ice made the river flow very fast. As they were going upstream, the water was flowing against them. Sometimes, the current was so strong they could not paddle their canoes forward. Then, they had to get out of their canoes and pull them. Often, they slipped on the wet rocks. They were also pricked by the sharp needles of a plant called the **cactus**.

▲ Grizzly bears are a large, dangerous type of brown bear. They can stand eight feet high. Lewis and Clark learned to be wary of grizzlies after one chased Lewis up a tree.

Then, the men came to a place where the river fell down over steep rocks. This **waterfall** forced them to take their canoes out of the water. They had found the Great Falls which are eighty feet high. The party now had to carry their supplies for twenty-five miles. They made carts on wheels called **wagons**, and then they cut a road through the forest. It took them a whole month to get past the Great Falls.

▼ Often, the men had to pull their boats through parts of the river where the current was too strong or where there were waterfalls.

By Horse through the Rockies

Lewis and Clark were now in the Rocky Mountains. The wagons they had made could not go across the steep mountain country. It looked as if they might have to turn back, but they would not give up.

Then, they had some luck. They met some Shoshone people. One of them was the brother of the young woman who had come with them as a guide. The Shoshone gave them some food and horses. Lewis and Clark continued with their journey. It got very cold as they climbed up into the mountains.

▲ Lewis and Clark were lucky to meet a group of Shoshone Indians. These were Sacajawea's relatives. They lived in the mountains and knew them well. "Shoshone" means "people of the valleys." These people told Lewis and Clark which route to follow through the mountains.

The Rockies and Beyond

Lewis and Clark moved along the high mountain paths, or **passes**, of the Rockies. They were getting short of food, and there were few animals to hunt in these high, cold places. At one time, they were so hungry they had to eat candles.

At last, the party was able to start climbing down from the Rockies. They found a village with friendly Nez Percé people. They gave Lewis and Clark fish and fresh meat. The men soon felt stronger, and they began to make new canoes. It was warmer away from the high mountain tops. The men got ready to continue their journey to the Pacific Ocean.

The Pacific Ocean

First, the men paddled along the Clearwater River. This river took them into the Snake River, and then into the Columbia River. The water flowed very fast. One canoe sank and the others were damaged. Often, the men had to stop on the sides, or **banks**, of the rivers to dry out their supplies. When they reached the Columbia River, they found high waves and waterfalls.

▼ An Indian encampment at the foot of the Rockies. The Nez Percé people fed dried lake salmon to Lewis and Clark's men. The men were also able to hunt again.

▼ On October 7, 1805, the travelers set out for the Pacific Ocean in their newly-built canoes.

In one place, it looked as if they would not be able to get through. Then, one of the men offered to take the canoes over the falls. He tied the canoes in pairs and paddled into the rough water. He managed to miss the rocks, but sometimes the other men could not see him in the spray of the waters. There was a great cheer when he reached the calm waters beyond.

After that, it was an easy journey to the sea. When he saw the Pacific Ocean, Clark wrote in his diary, "Ocean in view! O the joy!"

Winter by the Pacific Ocean

Lewis and Clark built a log fort on the shore of the ocean. They spent the winter there. Clark carved these words on a tall pine tree: "William Clark, 3 December 1805. By land, from the United States."

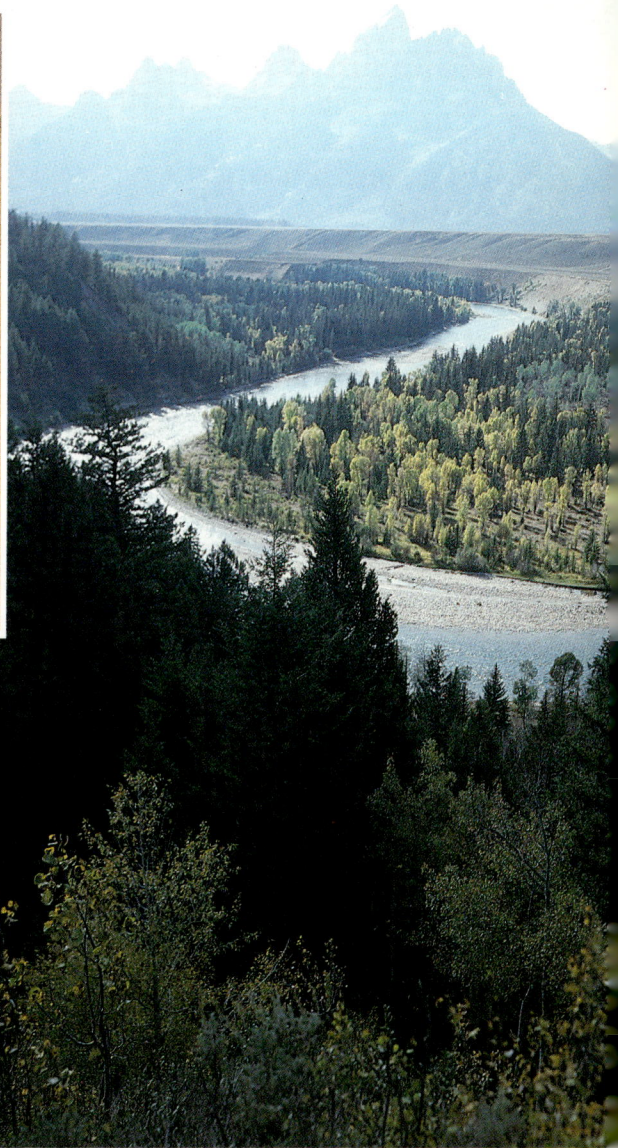

▲ The Snake River winds its way down from the Rocky Mountains to the Columbia River.

The winter passed slowly. It rained a lot, and they had only dried fish and meat to eat. The men knew the journey back would be hard, but they were glad to start off again in March, 1806.

Return to St. Louis

When Lewis and Clark started their return journey, they were 1,500 miles from St. Louis. This time, the waters of the Columbia River were against them. Their canoes were thrown against the rocks. They could not travel any longer on the river. Some local people gave them horses and food. Lewis and Clark wanted to find a shorter route than they had taken on their outward journey. The local people told them the best tracks, or **trails**, to follow.

▲ Lewis and Clark took different routes home. Clark went along the Yellowstone River. This area is now in the Yellowstone National Park.

By the end of June, the party had reached the valley of the Bitterroot River. Lewis and Clark wanted to explore as far as they could before getting back to St. Louis. The two men split up so that they could explore more places.

One group took a more northerly route and explored the Marias River. The other group went south and explored the Yellowstone region.

The Meeting with the Blackfoot

Lewis went with his group through a pass that is known today as the Lewis and Clark Pass. They went down the Sun River to the Great Falls. Then, the group headed across to the Marias River. There they met some of the Blackfoot people. Lewis asked eight of them to come and stay in his camp. During the night, one of the men woke up and saw the Blackfoot people running off into the darkness with their rifles and horses. Lewis killed two of them. There was no point after that in trying to explore the area. Lewis and his party had to try to escape from the lands of the Blackfoot. They covered over a hundred miles in twenty-four hours.

Lewis met Clark again on the Missouri. Clark had reached the Missouri with few problems. Both men traveled down the river towards St. Louis. On the way, they said goodbye to Sacajawea who had helped them so much.

▲ As Clark and his group traveled through the Yellowstone area, some Blackfoot Indians took their horses. They had to go the rest of the way by canoe.

Back in St. Louis

Lewis and Clark arrived in St. Louis to a great welcome. The journey had been a success. Lewis and Clark had been good leaders of their group. Only one person had died. The men had not found a way by river to the Pacific Ocean, but they had found vast new lands. These lands looked good for farming and hunting. The United States would now claim this area, and large numbers of farmers, herders, traders, and fur trappers would soon move there.

▼ The United States bought the Louisiana Territory from France in 1803. The Lewis and Clark expeditions had brought new knowledge back to the east about the area west of the Mississippi. The expedition's maps and charts helped the settlers who were moving west.

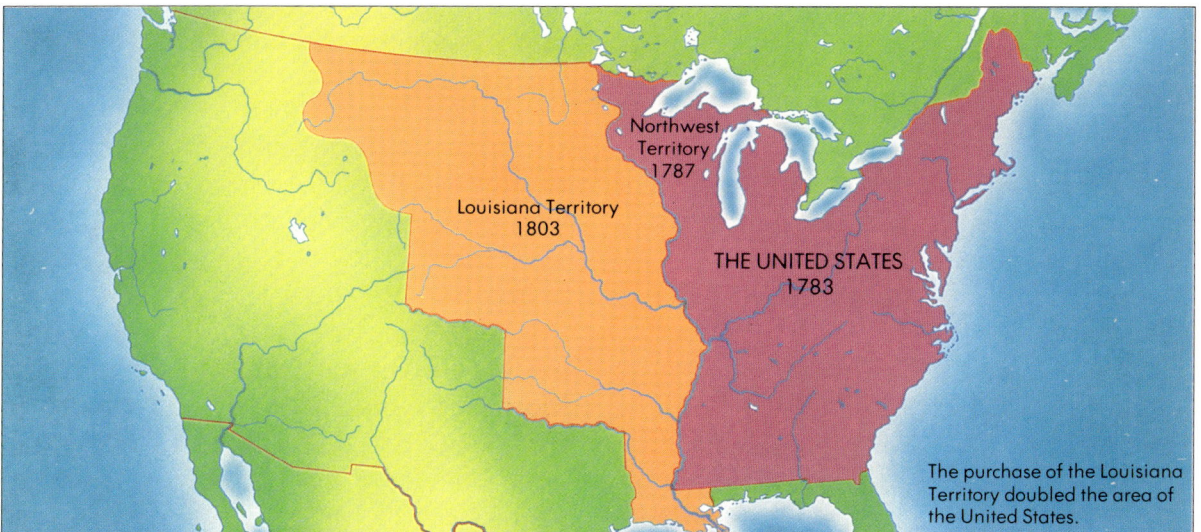

Northwest Territory 1787

Louisiana Territory 1803

THE UNITED STATES 1783

The purchase of the Louisiana Territory doubled the area of the United States.

A New Life in the West

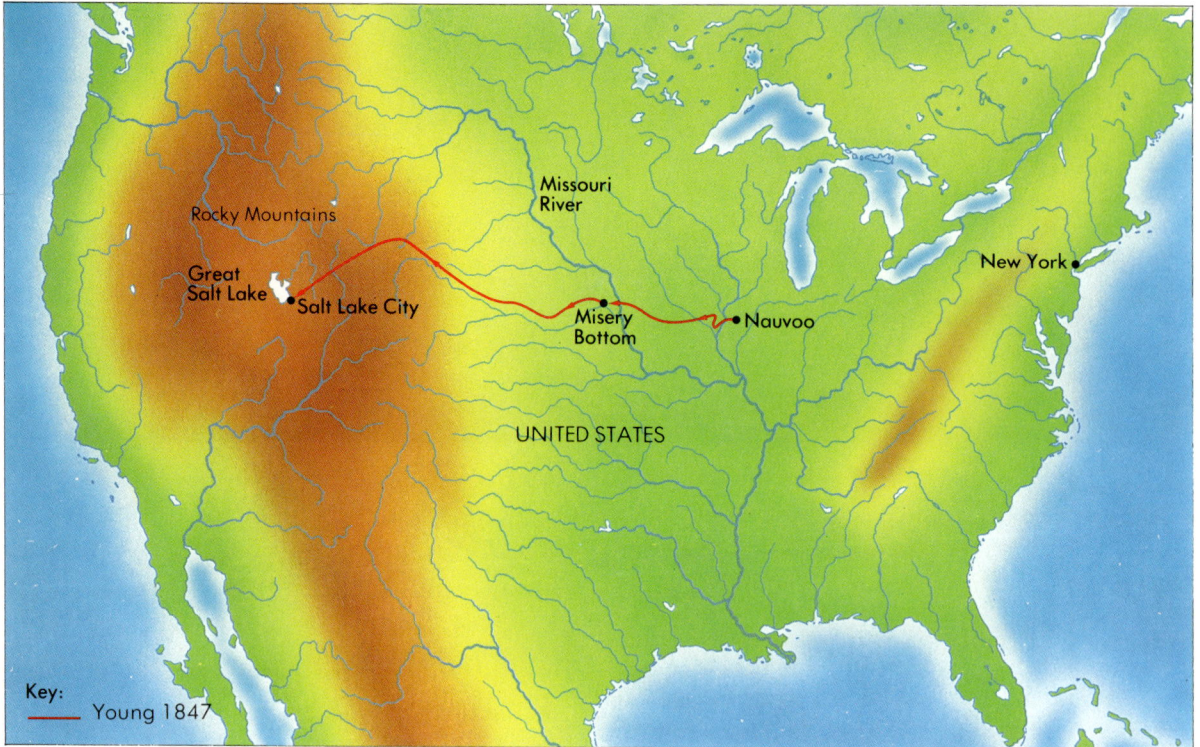

▲ The route Brigham Young and the Mormon people took to find a new home in the west.

After Lewis and Clark's journey, settlers in wagons moved across the United States to find good farming lands. Some people moved farther west into the forests and mountains. These were the fur trappers and traders.

Brigham Young

One man made a very different kind of journey. His name was Brigham Young. He was a follower of a man called Joseph Smith. Smith started the Mormon Church in 1830. Some people did not like this new faith. The Mormons were attacked, and they had to move westward. They went to Illinois, but people still attacked them. Their homes were burned down and their lives were in danger. Smith and his brother were put in prison, but in 1844, people broke into the prison and killed them both.

Brigham Young used to work in New York. He was a carpenter and painter. In 1832 he became a Mormon. When Smith was killed, the Mormons did not know what to do. They needed a strong leader to help them. Young was that person. In 1835, he became one of the twelve leaders of the new church. He said the Mormons would have to go far away to the west of the United States. There, they would be safe and could live as they wished.

▲ Joseph Smith, standing in the center, and the first leaders of the Mormon Church. Smith said that God had asked him to start a new religion. He also said that an angel told him where to find words from God, or scriptures, written on golden plates.

An Unusual Journey

Young was not an explorer like Marco Polo or Lewis and Clark. He was not looking for riches or new lands. He did not want to find a route to the Pacific Ocean. Young wanted to find a desert land which no one else wanted. In this land, his people could live in peace.

▶ This is the area in what is now Utah, where the Mormons decided to settle. In 1846, the area around the Great Salt Lake belonged to Mexico.

Young was told of an ideal place to take the Mormons. It was in the southern Rocky Mountains. This land was not yet part of the United States. It was the area around the Great Salt Lake. There was very little water and few trees. The lake itself was very salty, and the water was not fit for drinking or for crops. Young hoped that no one apart from Mormons would want to live there.

Journey to the Great Salt Lake

Brigham Young made careful plans for the journey. The Mormons had to work hard before moving to their new home. Each family had to prepare wagons and fill them with food and tools. Young first sent out a party of strong, young men. They took seeds and farm tools with them. They had to plant crops along the route to the Great Salt Lake. The main group of Mormons could then use these crops to feed themselves on their long journey west. The men also started to build houses, so that when the main group arrived, some houses would be ready to live in.

A Strong Leader

Young made up strict rules for the journey. The wagons had to form a circle at night. The day was also strictly planned. The families had to get up for prayers at 5:00 in the morning. Two hours later, the wagons would set off. The people had to keep in lines like soldiers on a march. After prayers at 8:30 in the evening, they all had to be in bed by 9:00.

▼ In the winter of 1846, the Mormons were forced to leave Nauvoo in Illinois.

▲ The Mormons camped by the Missouri River because they could not travel in midwinter.

The Great Salt Lake

At last, Young's group reached the Great Salt Lake. The land around it was hot and dry, and there was very little wood for fires. There was water in the mountain streams nearby, so the Mormons dug channels to make this water flow across their land. They built their houses from sundried bricks. The families shared the small amounts of food they could find. Soon, other Mormons joined them. In time, 80,000 people followed the first settlers. Some had pushed handcarts over 1,250 miles of rough ground. Later, towns grew up around the lake. The largest is Salt Lake City.

Although Young planned the journey very well, he could not stop people from dying of fever. Hundreds of Mormons died in low-lying land in the area around the Missouri River. The place was called "Misery Bottom."

Brigham Young died in 1877. He had found a new home and a new way of life for thousands of people in the west.

▼ When the Mormons reached the Great Salt Lake, Brigham Young looked down at the lake. and said, "This is the place." The Mormons knew that this was where they would settle forever.

Exploring Africa

In the early 1700's, people in Europe had little interest in Africa. The only people who went there were merchants. They bought gold, spices, ivory, and slaves at the trading centers on the coasts. People thought Africa was a hostile place with its thick jungles, wild animals, and unknown diseases.

The Unknown Land

At the end of the 1700's, many people wanted to find out more about Africa. Some groups wanted to know more about the rivers there, and if they could be used to find better trade routes. People had also heard of great riches in cities like Timbuktu.

Other groups also wanted to send people to Africa as **missionaries**. Many of these missionaries became explorers as well. One such person was David Livingstone.

David Livingstone

David Livingstone was born in Scotland in 1813. When he was ten years old, he went to work in a cotton mill. He had to work fourteen hours a day. After work, he studied at night. He wanted to become a doctor and work as a missionary in China. Then, he met a famous missionary named Robert Moffat, who had worked in Africa for many years. After speaking to Moffat, Livingstone decided to go to Africa instead.

In Kuruman

In 1840, Livingstone sailed for Cape Town at the southern tip of Africa. He traveled inland to Kuruman, a small village 600 miles to the north of Cape Town. Robert Moffat had worked in this area for twenty years. Livingstone was sad to find that few of the native people had become Christians in that time. He made several trips to the north of the village to try to **convert** more local people, but he had very little success.

Livingstone met Moffat's daughter, Mary, while he was at Kuruman. They got married and had children. Mary stayed with him to help him with his work.

Across the Kalahari

In 1849, Livingstone set out with two other men to search for Lake Ngami. They had heard it was to the north. To get there, they would have to cross the Kalahari Desert. No European had crossed this hot and dry desert before.

After crossing the Kalahari, the men turned northwest and at last came to Lake Ngami. This was to be the first of Livingstone's journeys which he made to learn more about Africa.

The following year, Livingstone set out northwards again. This time his wife and children traveled with him. During the journey, one of Livingstone's children died of a fever. After this, he decided to send his family back to Scotland. He wanted to explore more of Africa and continue his work.

◄ On one occasion, Livingstone was attacked by a lion as he prepared to shoot it. Although he escaped, his left arm was always weak because of the injury.

▼ Livingstone reached Lake Ngami in 1849. The lake lies to the north of the Kalahari Desert, in the country we now call Botswana. The Royal Geographical Society in London gave Livingstone a prize for this discovery.

Up the Zambezi

For many years, people in Africa had been taken from their homes and sold in foreign countries. Livingstone hated this cruel **slave trade** and wanted to stop it. He felt he could do this if he opened up new trade routes across Africa. This would bring in more settlers who could help to stop slavery.

Livingstone wanted to find a route into the middle of Africa which the traders could follow. He made a starting point, or **base**, at Linyanti. He left there in 1853 with twenty-seven Makololo people as porters and guides. He went up the Zambezi River. He wanted to explore the upper parts, or **reaches**, of the river. He hoped this might become a route for the traders. Some of the native people they met on their journey did not know what to think of Livingstone. Many of them had never seen a European before.

▲ During David Livingstone's journey up the Zambezi River, his boat was nearly overturned by the hippos several times.

On the Atlantic Coast

Livingstone found that the Zambezi River was not a good route towards the Atlantic Ocean. He had to leave the river and fight his way through the thick jungle. It took him six months to get to a town on the coast called Luanda. The Makololo people with him were amazed when they saw the ocean. They had never seen the sea before. They thought the land had no end.

▼ Livingstone had hoped to cross Africa by traveling along the Zambezi. He found that dangerous rapids and waterfalls made this impossible. These rapids are on the Zambezi at Tete in Mozambique.

Back to Linyanti

Livingstone was sick with fever when he reached the sea. In spite of this, he chose to go back overland. The journey back took a lot longer because Livingstone was still weak from his illness. It took one year to get back to Linyanti. Everybody was happy to see them. The Makololo were treated as heroes.

▶ David Livingstone kept a diary of his travels. He kept notes on the plants and animals he saw as well as the land he traveled through. In 1857, he published a book about his journeys in Africa. It was very popular, and 70,000 copies were sold.

Livingstone decided to stay in Linyanti for a few months to rest after his long journey. He also wanted to write notes and make maps of the area he had just explored. He was getting ready for a new journey. This time, he wanted to go down the Zambezi River to the Indian Ocean. He wondered if the route to the east coast would be better for traders.

The Crossing of Africa

In November, 1855, Livingstone left Linyanti to follow the Zambezi River to the Indian Ocean. After ten days, the men came to a place where the river fell over a high cliff.

Nobody from Europe had seen this waterfall before. It was 390 feet high and more than a mile wide. Livingstone named it "Victoria Falls" after the British queen. The Africans called the Falls of Mosioatunya "the smoke that sounds." The smoke was the cloud of spray which hung over the waterfall. The sound was the great noise made by the falling water. Livingstone wrote that it was "the most wonderful sight I ever saw in Africa."

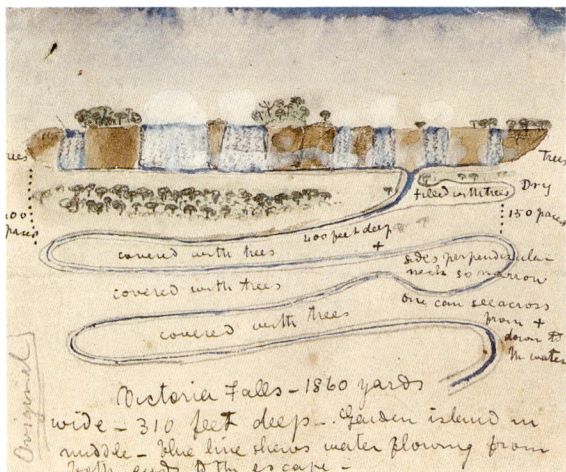

▲ David Livingstone drew this sketch of the Victoria Falls. The water drops into a deep, narrow chasm. Then, it flows through a winding gorge. The spray from the falls can be seen for many miles. Today, a statue of Livingstone stands at the Falls.

The Indian Ocean

Livingstone moved on down the Zambezi River to the east. He traveled about ten miles a day and made good progress. Many of the local people he met thought he was a slave trader. Livingstone told them that he was their friend and did not mean them any harm.

On May 20, 1856, Livingstone at last reached Quelimane. This is a small port near the northern part of the Zambezi **delta**, where the river flows into the Indian Ocean.

It had taken Livingstone two and a half years to cross the African continent from west to east. He was the first European ever to do so.

Return to Britain

Livingstone had been in Africa for sixteen years. He decided it was time to go back to Britain to see his family and friends. He was given a hero's welcome in Britain. He wrote a book about his travels and many people bought it.

Livingstone did not want to stay in Britain for long. The British people were very interested in his plan to open up a trading route along the Zambezi River. He was sent out to Africa again to look for trade routes and suitable places where people from Europe could live. This time his wife, Mary, went back with him.

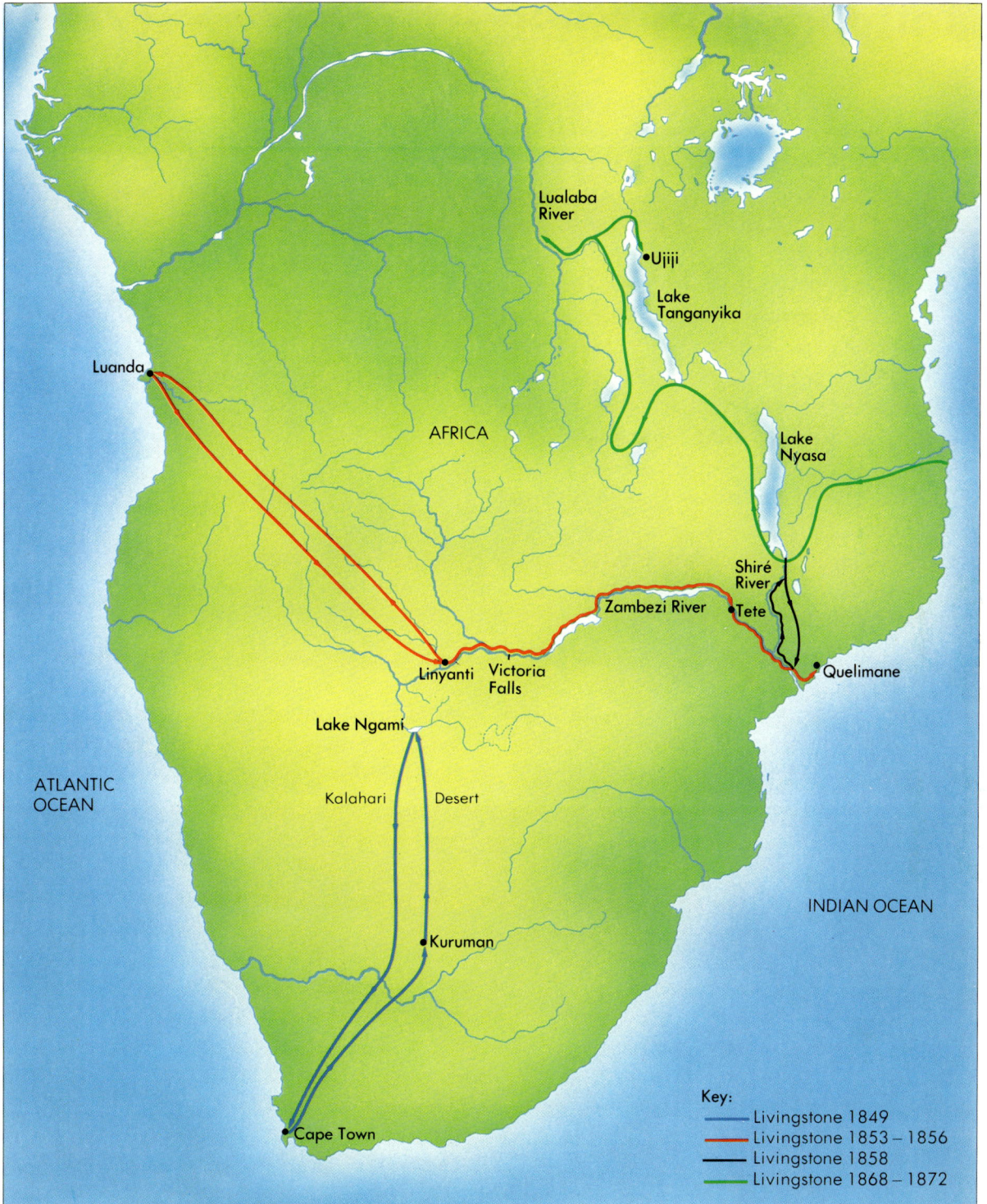

AFRICA

Lualaba
River

•Ujiji

Lake
Tanganyika

Luanda

Lake
Nyasa

Shiré
River

Zambezi River   •Tete

Linyanti   Victoria
Falls

Quelimane

Lake Ngami

ATLANTIC
OCEAN

Kalahari   Desert

INDIAN OCEAN

•Kuruman

Key:
Livingstone 1849
Livingstone 1853 – 1856
Livingstone 1858
Livingstone 1868 – 1872

•Cape Town

▲ David Livingstone traveled more than 30,000
miles during his journeys in Africa.

Journeys in East Africa

Livingstone set out for Africa again in 1858. There were seven people including his wife in his party. The sea journey was very difficult. The boat was very cramped and the crew became sick with fever. Livingstone did not get along well with the people in his party. He thought only of the journey ahead.

When the party reached the Zambezi, they found that the river was blocked by rapids. No boat could get past these rapids. Livingstone set off up the Shiré, which is one of the rivers that flows into the Zambezi. On the way, the party found a large lake called Lake Nyasa. They continued along the river, but more rapids blocked their way. Some of the people with him became very sick and his wife died of fever. Livingstone had to give up. He knew this was not a good route for traders, and in 1864 he decided to return to Britain.

The Last Journey

Livingstone stayed in Britain for one year. His last journey had been a failure. Now, he wanted to make new plans. He went back to Africa, but this time he was going to find where the Nile River started from. He wanted to find its **source**.

Livingstone's journey took him through East Africa, and farther north than he had ever been before. He was often very sick with fever. During one of his illnesses, Livingstone's medicine box was stolen and he thought he was going to die. Some Arab traders in Ujiji, a town on Lake Tanganyika, gave him food and medicine, and he got better.

▼ David Livingstone and his party camped for the night beside the Shiré River. The river flows from Lake Nyasa into the Zambezi River.

Meeting with Stanley

Livingstone set out again, and this time he found a river flowing north to the west of Lake Tanganyika. This was the Lualaba River. Sadly, it turned out that this river could not be a part of the Nile because it turned sharply to the west. He knew the Nile flowed north into Egypt. Livingstone returned again to Ujiji. He was very sick by this time. There, he met a young American journalist named Henry Stanley. Nobody had seen Livingstone for many years, and many were afraid he had died. Stanley had been sent to Africa by a New York City newspaper to try to find him. Stanley asked Livingstone to return to Britain, but he refused.

▼ Henry Stanley was sent by his newspaper to find Livingstone in 1871. Livingstone had been missing for many years. Many people thought he was dead. There is a story that Stanley shook Livingstone's hand when he met him and said, "Doctor Livingstone, I presume."

Soon after this meeting in 1873, Livingstone died. He was worn down by years of fever. His friends buried his heart in Africa as he had wished. His body was taken to Britain and buried in London.

▼ Livingstone had two special attendants named Chumah and Susi. They took care of him when he was sick, and carried him when he could not walk. After Livingstone died, they took his body to the coast, so that it could be sent home to Britain.

Mary Kingsley in Africa

Another famous explorer who traveled in Africa was Mary Kingsley. She was born in Britain in 1862. Her father was a doctor. He had been all around the world collecting rare birds and insects. Mary helped her father in his work and his writing.

▼ Mary Kingsley was one of the first women explorers. She went to Africa when her father died because she wanted to finish a book he was writing. She also wanted to work in a hot tropical area and find out about the people who lived there.

Mary was thirty years old when her father died. She decided to carry on her father's life work. She had read about West Africa, and she chose this area to carry on the study of birds and insects.

Travels in West Africa

Mary traveled to West Africa in 1893. She took very few things with her on her journey. She had only one bag with books, some boots, a few clothes, and a blanket.

▼ When Mary Kingsley traveled, she had to use local transportation. There was no other way to get from place to place. This is the canoe that she used to go up the Ogowe River in West Africa. Three types of fish that she found on her travels were later named after her.

Mary arrived in Accra on the west coast. She started off with some local porters and guides, and traveled through the thick forests. She also went by canoe along the rivers. Often, the rivers were wide and shallow. Crocodiles were a great danger. One nearly upset her canoe. Mary took a paddle and banged it on the nose! The crocodile gave up and swam away.

Mary collected many birds, insects, and fish on her first trip. She took some back to Britain. The British were so pleased with what she had found that they gave her money to return to West Africa in order to continue her work.

Return to Africa

In 1894, Mary returned to West Africa. This time, she went to places where nobody from Europe had been before. She explored the Ogowe River, and spent five months studying wild life in that area. Then, she went into the land of the Fang, who were very fierce people. She spent a week among them. Although they were curious, they were not hostile towards her.

Once on her travels, Mary fell into a deep hole. It had been dug by the native people to catch animals, and there were sharp sticks at the bottom. Her guides pulled her out. Mary's thick skirts had saved her, and she was lucky not to have been hurt.

Mary Kingsley returned to Britain, and she published a book called *Travels in West Africa* in 1897. Three years later, she went to South Africa to nurse soldiers in the **Boer War**. She caught a fever while she was working in the hospital, and died in June, 1900. Mary had asked to be buried at sea. She was only thirty-eight years old when she died.

▼ The area Mary Kingsley traveled through in West Africa.

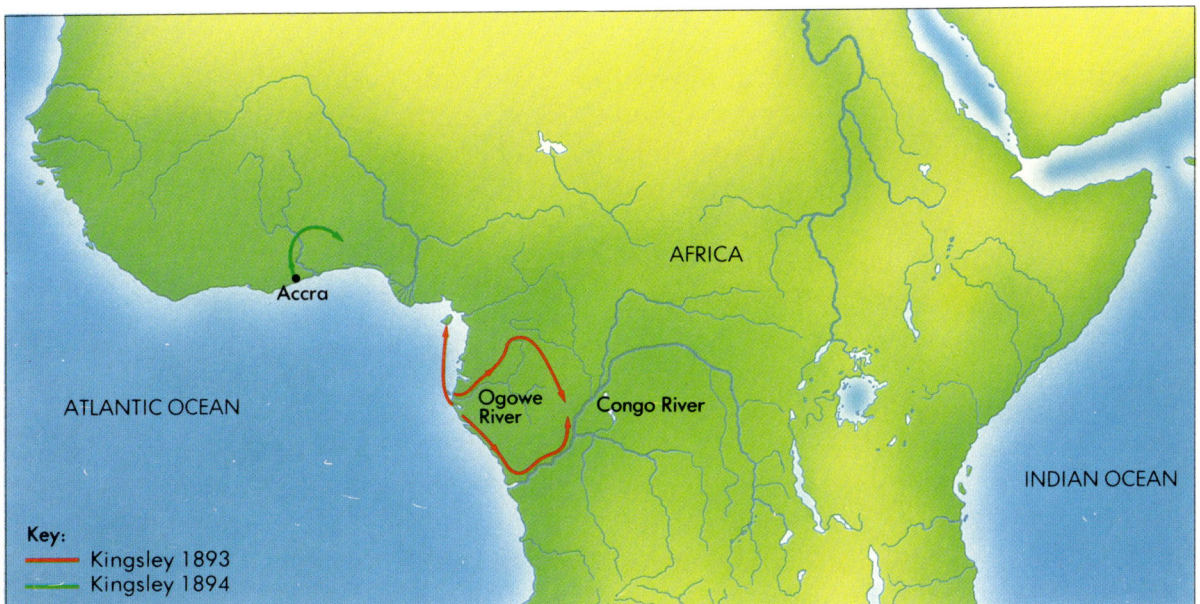

Key:
— Kingsley 1893
— Kingsley 1894

AFRICA

ATLANTIC OCEAN

Accra

Ogowe River

Congo River

INDIAN OCEAN

Travels in the Middle East

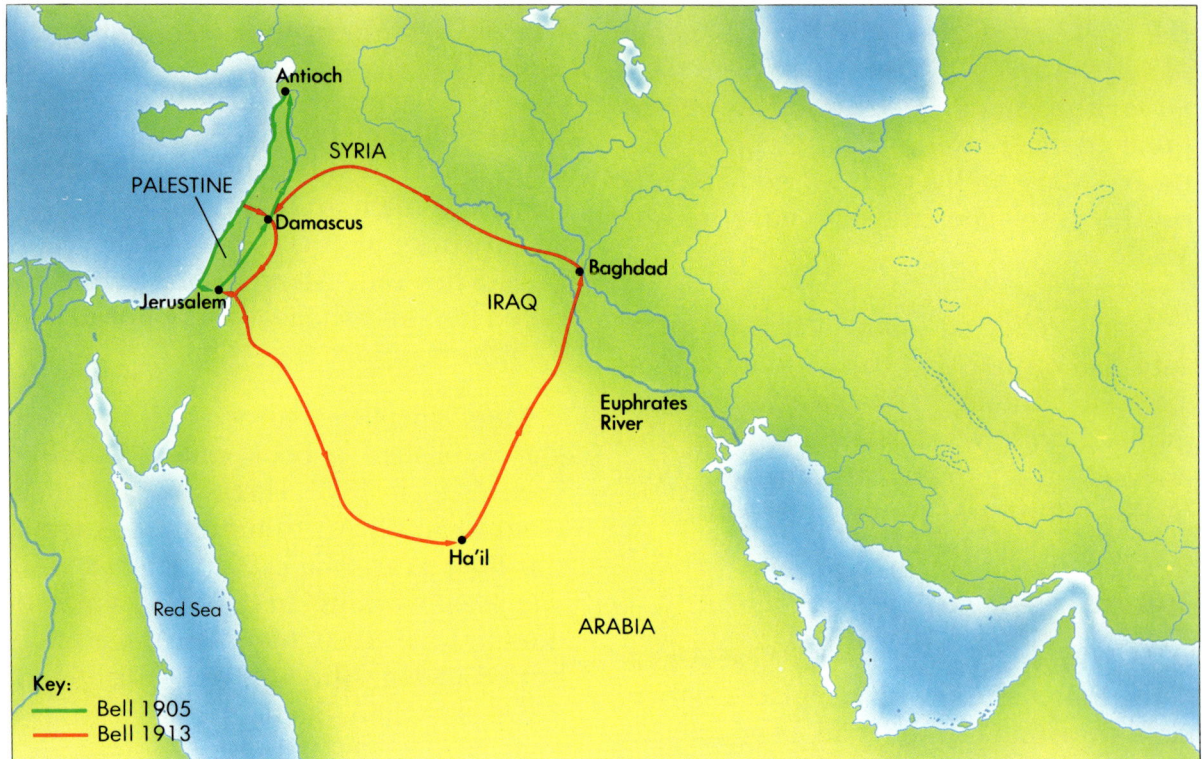

Map showing Antioch, SYRIA, PALESTINE, Damascus, Jerusalem, Baghdad, IRAQ, Euphrates River, Ha'il, Red Sea, ARABIA

Key:
— Bell 1905
— Bell 1913

▲ Gertrude Bell visited many countries in the Middle East during her life.

By the beginning of the 1900's, most of the areas of the world had been mapped and explored. However, there were still a few remote lands where few people had traveled. There were also mountains to be climbed. During the last eighty years, travelers and climbers have visited these remote places.

One such person was Gertrude Bell. She was born in Britain in 1888, and studied at a college in Oxford. She wanted to travel to countries in the Middle East, so she learned to speak Arabic, Persian, and Turkish.

Gertrude was a very fit person who liked outdoor sports. She became a climber and climbed many mountains in Switzerland in the early 1900's.

Adventures in Syria

Gertrude's first journey was in 1905. She set out from Jerusalem in what was then **Palestine** to cross the sandy deserts and plains of Syria. In many places, people stared at her. They had never seen a European before. She visited many of the old cities like Damascus and Antioch.

In Syria, Gertrude met some people called the Druze. The Druze were a proud people, and they did not mix with other people in the area. They liked and respected Gertrude. Once, when she approached one of their villages, she heard the sound of guns being fired. She thought she might be killed, but the shots were fired to welcome her!

Adventures in Arabia

In 1913, Gertrude went on a journey to Arabia. There are vast, sandy deserts there. Gertrude sometimes started her travels at 2:00 in the morning to avoid traveling in the middle of the day when it was very hot.

While Gertrude was in Arabia, she visited the secret city of Ha'il. She was only the second European woman to visit this city. The first was Anne Blunt, who had traveled in the Arabian Desert with her husband in the 1870's.

▼ Gertrude Bell worked for Sir Percy Cox while he was the British High Commissioner in Iraq. In this picture, she is with Sir Percy and Ibn Saud. Ibn Saud later became King of Saudi Arabia.

Gertrude got to know Arabia and its people very well. In World War I, from 1914 to 1918, the British Army asked her to go back there. They needed her advice on its people and customs.

Gertrude spent the last years of her life in Baghdad in Iraq. She was working in the National Museum of Iraq until her death in 1926.

▼ Gertrude Bell settled in Baghdad, the capital of Iraq. Baghdad lies on the Euphrates River. This is what it looks like today.

Freya Stark

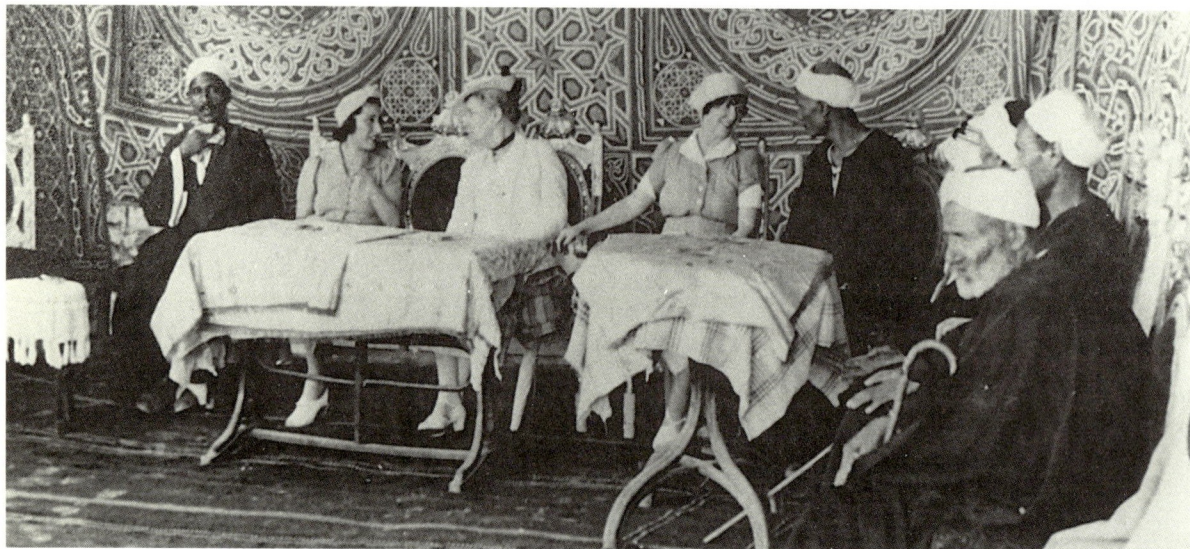

▲ Freya Stark traveled all over the Arab world. She wrote many books about her travels. This photograph of Freya Stark was taken while she lived in Cairo. She is seated fourth from the left.

Freya Stark was born in Britain in 1892. She spent some of her childhood in the Alps in northern Italy. Then, she joined her father who had a fruit farm in Canada. Freya always wanted to travel. Above all, she wanted to go to the Middle East. During her lifetime, Freya spent over thirty years traveling in this area. She visited many countries like Iraq, Syria, Persia, Jordan, and Turkey. She wrote many books about the people she met and the places she saw.

Travels from Baghdad

In 1929, Freya went to Baghdad in Iraq. From that city, Freya was to make most of her journeys over the next thirty years. On one of her trips, Freya went to "The Valley of the Assassins." Marco Polo had given this name to the valley in the 1200's. When he passed through that valley many hundreds of years before, strangers were often killed by the people who lived there. When Freya went there in 1930, it was very different. She saw only one man with a gun. The people were kind, and they let her sleep in their homes. In one village, all the families slept on the roof of one house because it was too hot to sleep inside their homes.

Once Freya became very sick with fever up in a mountain village. She thought she was going to die. For five days, she lay on a rough bed. She was afraid to drink the water because it was dirty. She had only sour milk to drink and the white of an egg to eat. She did get better, but she caught fever again many more times. In spite of this, she continued with her travels.

▲ Freya Stark in Saudi Arabia. She went there after she made her first trip to Luristan. She wrote two books about her travels in Saudi Arabia.

In Luristan

Freya made two journeys to an area east of Baghdad called Luristan. Today, the area is part of Iran. At that time, it was a remote and dangerous place. She thought she would be robbed, so she took very little with her. She took no guns because she was sure the people would try to take them from her. One man wanted to take her hat. She stopped him by saying he would look silly wearing a lady's hat!

On her second journey in 1932, Freya went to an even more remote part of Luristan. In one village, she was attacked by dogs. The people were very sorry. Freya did not want to upset them. She was in great pain, but she did not complain.

Like Gertrude Bell, Freya Stark was asked to help the British Army during World War I. She went back to the Alps in Italy to retire, and remained active well into her nineties.

▲ Freya Stark in the garden of her home in Italy. When she grew old, she spent most of her time in Italy. She did not, however, give up traveling. When she was 83, she went on a journey down the Euphrates River.

Mount Everest

Mount Everest is the highest mountain in the world. It is one of a group of very high mountains called the Himalayas. They are to the north of India in Nepal and Tibet. They are so high that it is always very cold on the mountain tops. They are always covered with snow and ice.

Everest is nearly 30,000 feet above the level of the sea. That is more than five and a half miles high. One of the gases in the air is **oxygen**. There is not much of this gas in the air when you climb very high. This makes it difficult to breathe on high mountains. People have to take oxygen with them in tanks, which they carry on their backs.

Early Climbers on Mount Everest

People have always wanted to climb to the top, or **summit**, of Mount Everest. Seven groups of British climbers tried to climb the mountain in the 1920's and 1930's. They were helped a lot by the Sherpa people who live in the mountains. The Sherpas helped the climbers to find their way and carried their food, tents and tanks of oxygen.

In 1952, some Swiss climbers almost reached the top. They were only 750 feet from the top, but they were so tired and so cold that they had to turn back. A Sherpa named Tenzing Norgay was with the Swiss climbers. He learned a lot about the highest parts of Everest.

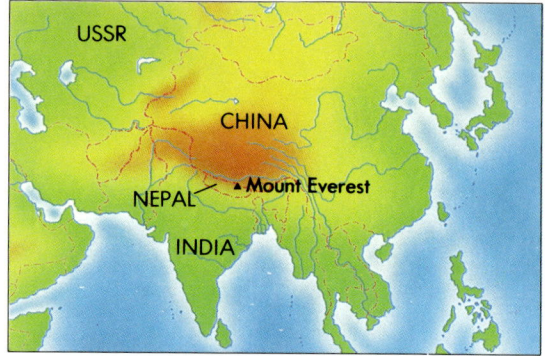

▲ The highest mountain in this picture is Mount Everest. It is 29,028 feet high. The local name for the mountain is Chomo-Langma. This means "Goddess Mother of the World." In the 1830's, the mountain was named after Sir George Everest, Surveyor-General of India. He did a lot of exploring and mapmaking in India.

The Top At Last

In 1953, Tenzing Norgay joined a party of British climbers led by John Hunt. After a long climb, they made a camp just below the summit. On May 28, 1953, Norgay and a New Zealand climber named Edmund Hillary set out to try to reach the summit itself. It was a slow and hard climb, and they had to use their oxygen. They made a camp that night on a narrow shelf that they cut out of the ice. Early in the morning, they moved on, slowly upwards. At last, they stood on the summit. They were the first people to stand on the highest place in the world.

Since 1953, many people have climbed Everest. In 1963, an American group climbed to the top by a new route, and then came down a different way. In 1975, a group of Japanese women climbed the mountain and one of them, Junko Tabei, reached the summit.

Although many people have now stood on the summit of Everest, the mountain is still dangerous and a challenge to climbers from all over the world.

▲ In 1953, the British Expedition went up Mount Everest from the south. Experts had thought that this was impossible. The camp in the picture is the base camp, at about 16,250 feet up. Climbers took supplies up another 9,750 feet. Edmund Hillary and Tenzing Norgay set off for the summit from there.

▲ Because it is very cold on Mount Everest, Tenzing Norgay and Edmund Hillary had to wear special clothing to keep them warm. They also carried oxygen with them because the air is so thin. When they reached the summit, they stayed there for fifteen minutes.

A Journey across Australia

Ernest Giles made the first crossing of the western deserts of Australia in 1876. He went with horses and mules and crossed from Alice Springs, a town in the center, to the Indian Ocean. Today, the deserts remain an empty area, but the journey is made by air or by jeep. The land routes that exist are bumpy and difficult. It is easy to get lost or break down faraway from help. One person wanted to cross this dry and dusty area in a different way. This person's name is Robyn Davidson.

The Camel Lady

Robyn Davidson was born in Australia in 1950. She grew up on a huge cattle farm, or **station**, in an area of Australia called Queensland. She loved the outdoor life.

Robyn was twenty-five years old when she planned her long journey. She wanted to walk from the center of Australia to the west coast. This area is very hot and dry. There are some wild camels in Australia. These camels are hard to catch and train. Robyn wanted to use camels to carry her supplies on her journey. At last, she trained three camels. Then, one of them had a baby, so Robyn set off with four camels across the Gibson Desert.

In April, 1977, Robyn left Alice Springs. She took her dog Diggity with her. Flies and ants bothered her a lot. Other wild camels were also a danger. Once, she had to fire her gun in the air to scare away a herd of forty camels.

▼ Robyn Davidson traveled with four camels and her dog Diggity.

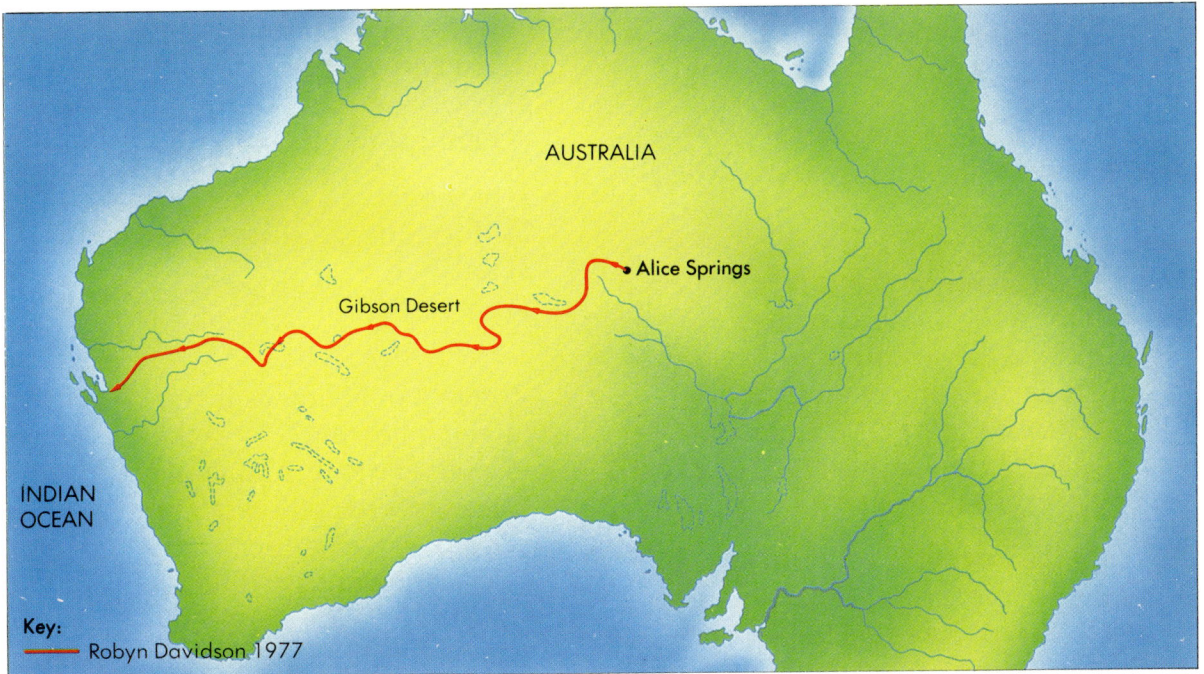

AUSTRALIA

Alice Springs

Gibson Desert

INDIAN
OCEAN

Key:
Robyn Davidson 1977

▲ The route Robyn Davidson took from Alice Springs, to the west coast.

Robyn crossed sandhills and huge plains of yellow grass. People called **Aborigines** live in this area. They are **nomads**, people who move around looking for food and water. She met an old Aborigine man named Eddie. He walked with her for 200 miles, and he taught her to find and eat food which the Aborigines had learned to survive on in the desert. Robyn's skin became dark and tough like leather. She had one very sad moment when her dog Diggity died. He ate some poison which had been put down to kill wild dogs, or **dingoes**. She had lost a good friend.

When Robyn's journey was over, she found a good home for her camels on a cattle station on the west coast. They had served her well on her 1,700 mile journey.

▼ At last, Robyn and the camels reached the west coast. They all enjoyed a cool bathe in the Indian Ocean at the end of their long journey.

Land Travelers

We have looked at explorers from different times who explored different areas. They all had two things in common. They had courage, and they were willing to face the unknown. These people opened up new lands in many continents, and it is through their efforts that we know so much about our world today.

Quiz

How much can you remember. Try this quiz. Use the index and glossary to help you find the answers.

1. Here are some famous land travelers with the letters of their names scrambled. Unscramble the letters to find their correct names.
   a) ZIEKENMAC, b) NOUGY, c) KARST, d) OAMRC LOPO, e) ZNETING, f) ONESTINGVIL, g) SIWEL

2. Write the following sentences on a separate sheet of paper. Then, fill in the blank spaces using the words in the box below.
   a) David _____ was an early explorer in _____.
   b) He explored the Zambezi _____ by _____ and on foot.
   c) He reached the _____ Ocean and then crossed to the Indian Ocean.
   d) He was the first European to see the _____ Falls.
   e) He died in _____, and was buried in _____.

Crockett, New York, Asia, tunnel, Victoria, spice, 1869, car, River, Pacific, Africa, 1873, London, canoe, Atlantic, Niagara, Islam, Livingstone

3. Match the descriptions given in (a) to (e) with the words numbered (1) to (5) below them.
   a) The capital city of the Mongol Empire
   b) The junction of the Mississippi and Missouri
   c) Followers of Joseph Smith
   d) An African desert
   e) The American who found Livingstone at Ujiji

   1) St. Louis
   2) Mormons
   3) Kalahari
   4) Stanley
   5) Cambuluc

4. Where would you be if you were in or on the following?
   a) a secret city in Arabia
   b) a river with a hissing noise, like the voice of evil spirits
   c) a lake with salty water and very few trees around it
   d) a place which the African people called the "smoke that sounds"
   e) the top of the world, in the Himalayas

5. Complete the following sentences with (a), (b), (c) or (d):

   1) Paper money and printing began in
      a) Venice.
      b) Ceylon.
      c) China.
      d) India.

   2) Joseph Smith was killed while in
      a) Salt Lake City.
      b) New York.
      c) hiding.
      d) prison.

   3) The early traders on the coast of Africa wanted
      a) gold and ivory.
      b) sugar and cotton.
      c) tea and coffee.
      d) woollen goods.

4) One explorer who was saved by
   her thick skirts was
   a) Robyn Davidson.
   b) Gertrude Bell.
   c) Mary Kingsley.
   d) Freya Stark.

5) Alice Springs is in the center of
   a) Africa.
   b) America.
   c) Australia.
   d) Asia.

6. How many land explorers can you
   find with names beginning with
   L and S?

7. Who or what
   a) ruled the Mongol Empire?
   b) made the first overland crossing of
      North America?
   c) is the name of the large bear found
      in the Rockies?
   d) wanted to settle his Mormon
      people in a desert land?
   e) visited a village of the Druze people
      in Syria?

8. Are these statements true or false?
   a) The first explorers were mainly
      merchants.
   b) Kublai Khan ate off gold dishes.
   c) Mackenzie wore animal hides to
      protect himself against the cold.
   d) The Columbia River flows into the
      Atlantic Ocean.
   e) Livingstone was attacked by a
      leopard and badly injured.

9. Are the following islands, rivers or
   lakes?
   a) Java
   b) Superior
   c) Peace
   d) Clearwater
   e) Ngami
   f) Nyasa (Malawi)
   g) Tanganyika
   h) Zambezi
   i) Nile
   j) Sumatra

Answers

1. a) MACKENZIE b) YOUNG, c) STARK,
   d) MARCO POLO, e) TENZING,
   f) LIVINGSTONE, g) LEWIS

2. (a) Livingstone, Africa, (b) River, canoe,
   (c) Atlantic, (d) Victoria, (e) 1873, London

3. (a) 5, (b) 1, (c) 2, (d) 3, (e) 4

4. (a) Ha'il, (b) Mackenzie River, (c) Salt
   Lake, (d) Victoria Falls, (e) Mount
   Everest

5. 1 (c), 2 (d), 3 (a), 4 (c), 5 (c)

6. Lewis, Livingstone, Stanley, Stark

7. (a) Kublai Khan, (b) Mackenzie,
   (c) grizzly, (d) Brigham Young,
   (e) Gertrude Bell

8. (a) true, (b) true, (c) true, (d) false,
   (e) false

9. (a) Island, (b) Lake, (c) River, (d) River,
   (e) Lake, (f) Lake, (g) Lake, (h) River,
   (i) River, (j) Island

Glossary

Aborigine: the name given to the people who originally lived in Australia. It comes from a latin word meaning "from the beginning."

bank: a raised slope of earth along the edge of a river, road, or lake.

base: a place from which an organization or expedition works and keeps its main supplies.

blacksmith: a person who makes items from heated iron by hammering and beating the iron into shape.

Boer War: the war fought between the British by the Boer settlers in South Africa from 1899 to 1922.

cactus: a spiney plant which is found in dry, desert areas. Often, cactuses have large brightly-colored flowers.

canal: a water channel built across land to join two bodies of water. Canals are also built to improve the course of a river and drain the land.

caravan: a group of people and their camels traveling across the desert.

Ceylon: an island in the Indian Ocean which is off the southeast coast of India. The name of the island was changed to Sri Lanka in 1972.

continent: a large piece of land, sometimes including many countries. Earth is divided into seven continents.

convert: to cause somebody to change their beliefs, faith, or opinion.

court: the main dwelling or household of a ruler or nobleman from which the ruler governs.

current: the flow of water within a sea, lake, or river.

delta: a fan-shaped area of land made by the mud, sand, and stones dropped at a river mouth. The river divides into many channels as it flows through the delta to the sea.

dingo: a wild dog found in Australia. The dog has a yellowish-brown coat and looks like a wolf.

East: the countries of Asia. Asia was often called the East because travelers coming from Europe journeyed eastwards to get there.

emperor: someone who rules or reigns over an empire.

empire: several countries or groups of people all ruled by one government.

fort: a strong building used for defense.

frontier: the edge of a country or the farthest point that has been explored in a new land.

missionary: a person sent out by a religious group to convert other people to their own faith or beliefs.

mouth: the place where a river flows into the sea.

nation: a large group of people, usually with their own government and language.

nomad: someone who moves from place to place in search of food or to find grass for animals. Nomads do not make their homes in any one particular place.

Northwest Passage: a shipping route from the Atlantic Ocean to the Pacific Ocean across North America.

oxygen: a gas found in air and water. Oxygen is very important to all plants and animals. We cannot breathe without oxygen.

Palestine: the name for the historic area between the Jordan River and the Mediterranean Sea. It is now the country of Israel.

party: a group of people working or taking part in an activity together.

pass: a narrow path, road, or track between mountains.

pavilion: one of a set of buildings which makes up a bigger building. A pavilion is usually highly decorated.

Persia: a country in the Middle East now called Iran. Once, it had an ancient empire which stretched from Egypt to India.

rapids: a part of a river where the water flows very fast over rocks. The water is usually shallow, so the rocks make the water very rough.

reach: a stage of a river. The stage near the beginning of a river is called the upper reach.

remote: describes something which is far away or distant. A remote island is a long way from other land.

route: the way to get from one place to another. Routes are shown on maps and plans.

slave trade: the business of buying and selling people, especially the trade of slaves from Africa to America from the 1500's to the 1800's.

source: the place where something begins. The source of a river can be a spring or a lake.

station: a name for a large farm, such as a cattle or sheep ranch in Australia.

summit: the highest point or part of a mountain.

tablet: a piece of stone or wood used to write on in ancient times.

trade: to do business by buying and selling goods.

trail: a road or track across wild country.

trapper: a person who traps wild animals, especially for their furs or hides.

waterfall: a part of a river where water falls straight down over a cliff.

Index